The Light Within

selected poetry of

Thomas Ray Marshall

© 2003 by Thomas Ray Marshall. All rights reserved.

No part of this book may be reproduced, stored in a retrieval system, or transmitted by any means, electronic, mechanical, photocopying, recording, or otherwise, without written permission from the author.

ISBN: 1-4107-5653-X (e-book)
ISBN: 1-4107-5652-1 (Paperback)
ISBN: 1-4107-5651-3 (Dust Jacket)

Library of Congress Control Number: 2003093321

This book is printed on acid-free paper.

Printed in the United States of America
Bloomington, IN

1stBooks – rev. 10/03/03

To my dad, Weck, who fired the
ember, and to Nancy, who
fans the flame.

There is a rhythm in nature that is imitated in art. It is felt and heard in the wind, the light of sun and shadow, the pulsing of blood, the cadence of a walk, the meter of breathing. Poetry emanates from these vibrations as the word, rhythmically pulsating with a cadence and a meter.

Table of Contents

Snapshot 1
Sunday Morning 2
On The Green 3
The Poet and the Flower 5
Computerage 7
The Inheritance 8
Take Life 9
Of Head and Heart 10
On The Porch 11
Now Nancy 12
Sanctuary 13
American Farewell 14
Love Is 15
Maple Tree 16
The Last Ride 18
Pine Glen 19
I Want To Be 20
Geography Class 21
First Birth 23
Building a Nation 24
Out of Paris 25
Dylan 27
A Card Played 28
Aging 30
At Last 31
Fire of the Soul 32
Aurora Borealis 33
Closing Time 34
Sentinel Cedars 35

Ecumenical Ox	36
A Chilling Freeze	37
The Rose Room	38
Patriotic Pubs	39
Frankfort, Michigan	40
Uniquely Me	41
Man of the Planet	42
Kassie's Song	45
Song of Ruth	46
Nancy In Ireland	47
The Bomb	48
River of Intensity	49
Mozart at Night	50
Annie B. and Nick	51
Magical Land	52
Reconciliation	53
Autumn	54
Two Surprises	55
War and Sacrifice	56
Dissipating Grief	57
Christmas Child	58
Summer at the Lake	59
Autobiographically Less Than One Hundred Words	63
Let Your Heart Lead the Way	64
I See You on the Fourth of July	65
Fifty Years and Less	66
As Catbirds Do	68
Missing You	69
Community Porch	70
When You're Away	71
Dreams Kilarney	72

Death of a Young Boy 73
Crow 74
Beneath The Veil 75
Past Paradise 76
Balance 78
Vernal Equinox 79
Hitting the Road 80
Just a Little Girl and Me 81
October 83
Retirement 84
My Blue Canoe 86
Photographs 87
The Periwinkle Prayer 90
Love 91
Former Wife 92
April 93
Inconstant Heart 94
After Life 95
A Public House 96
Eternity 97
Fading Dreams 98
Road to Success 99
Angel's Song 100
Winter Wore This Year 101
Your Beauty 102
Do Not Despair 103
Compromise 104
The Lady 105
Heroes 106
Forever Together 107
Fifteen Years 108

Near Your Bed	109
How Sad Her Death	110
Orbit	111
Religious Air	112
Tunnel of Love	114
Day After Day	115
The Light Within	118
To Build a Wall	119
Vacation	120
My Legacy	122
Nancy's Birthday	123
Approaching the Storm	124
Raven	126
National Ways	127
Kassie Lee	128
Insight	129
Love's Return Home	130
The Snake is an "S"	132
Twenty Years	133
Cats of Peace	134
Andrew's Visit	135
Intrusion	138
Giving In	139
Not Today	140
We Come Again	141
Sweet Recall	142
Song Too Short	143
Anticipation	144
Before She Wakes	145
The Trio	147
Uncle Tom is Dead	148

Divorce	150
At Present	151
Discontentment	152
Respectful Timing	153
The Promise	155
Two Brothers and a Wife	156
Not April	158
Night Thoughts	159
A Letter Inside a Book	161
Sunday	162
Life's ABC's	163
Religion	164
Summer Thunder	165
Last Good-byes	166
Toward Motherhood	167
Stars	168
Emily Dickinson	169
Henry and the Angels	170
Sheltered Sin	173
Moving Away	174
I Thought Life Cruel	175
Mockingbird	176
Fallout	177

Snapshot

Where floats our life
when we look out to sea?
What turns the tide, and how?
We ebb and flow as memory
escaping from the now.
A swimmer in a pinafore,
a wink, a blink in time.
A snapshot on a static shore,
a frozen pantomime.

Sunday Morning

Your laugh rings from the garden
As the church bell rings the town.
You stand with Suze and priestly glads
And chat the morning round.

Your fading voices float toward grace
In streams of garden talk,
Japonica and coreopsis
Bouncing in your walk.

Then you are cloistered in the church
With sacred wine and host
While I seek some religion
In my coffee cup and toast.

Too soon will come the day
When earthly rituals will pass,
The planting of a garden,
The chanting of a mass.

I pray my final day will be
Along your garden path,
In tune with the vibrations of
The church bell and your laugh.

On The Green

Forever laced in leggings, with
A helmet in his hand,
O'Mally marched from World War One,
And will forever stand
In tribute to the Irishmen,
Who for their country died.
But now birds perch upon his head,
And children by his side.

And children sit across the green
Upon a poet's knee,
Where he creates his granite verse
For future history.
And down through generations long,
With lateral regard,
We build our marble tributes to
The soldier and the bard.

And though the soldiers' weapons change,
And likely will again,
The only weapon wielded by
The poet is a pen.
And he will always write of the
Atrocities of war,
While parliaments will propagate
And send their plans afar,

Making other nations safe
For our democracy,
Forming other cultures as
We think they ought to be.
Call home the soldier. Take his gun.
Have his commander know it.
It is our hope to have, henceforth,
Our hero be a poet.

From now on any marble we
Erect upon the square
Will be to honor hope instead
Of consummate despair.
From now on any bird or child,
With equally free will
May perch upon the granite of
A tablet and a quill.

The Poet and the Flower

A syncopated life they lived,
The poet and the flower.
They floated from the sunny field
Into the shady bower.
Their radiance was ever bright,
Each living in the one.
They danced from darkness into light,
Onto the field of sun.
He weaved his words into a phrase.
She planted in the earth.
It was their law to spin their straw
To artifacts of worth.
They waded streams, they slept in dreams.
In peace their day would break.
They walked the beach and sheltered each
From danger and heartache.

Their love flowed out to everyone,
Their radius entire,
Inviting old and hurt and cold
To gather round their fire.
They never knew a cloudless day,
Though clouds to them were gain.
When storms would break, you'd see them take
Their troubles to the rain.
They asked for nature's intervene.
They felt the season's kiss.
They taught the same to young who came
To shed a chrysalis.

Their open hospitality
Upon their sacred ground
Provided rest for any guest
Till morning rolled around

Sincerity was in their smiles,
Their manner not contrived.
They fanned a soft religious flame,
Their spirits not deprived.
And when their final embers died,
Their ash was mixed as one,
Eternal union, sanctified,
The way it had begun.
Their life was just a common life,
Endowed with ample power.
Their love was but a basic love,
The poet and the flower.

Computerage

The Royal and the Underwood creation
Saw me through my higher education;
Thirty years of legal cap and pen,
And then one morning William Gates dropped in!
Progressive magic, yes, but quite absurd
To look in windows for the perfect word.
The perfect word was still inside my head,
Awaiting inspiration to be said.
The World Book or the Bible or a quip
Embodied in a silver microchip
That in a decade would be legislative
Regarding Microsoft and the creative
Mind would have to make a choice
To write like Stephen King or Keats and Joyce.
The word henceforth would never be the same.
To read my mail I'd have a coded name.
They tried in vain to show me how much better
It was to never write a longhand letter.
"You may as well sit still and take your tonic.
From now on words will all be electronic."
Well, that was fine if it would stop the speaking,
But that was not the answer they were seeking.
They wanted me to put away my scribe
And use the "…mouse and keyboard packed inside."
So as they sold more computech utensils,
I started hoarding pens and pads and pencils.
The computer that was balanced on my spine
Would serve me in my waning years just fine.
I may be older than a pterodactyl,
But with a pen in hand it's just more tactile.

The Inheritance

A somber knell, the final bell,
To summon heirs around,
Anticipating fortune in
The melancholy sound.
Her darkened room is like a tomb,
With matriarchal bed,
Sweet scented lilies lacquering
The rancor of the dead.
Third cousins touch third cousins, as
The living still embrace.
A silver service sparkles on
A cloth of Belgium lace.
Two Ming prayer jugs, four Persian rugs,
Carved ivory, a Matisse,
All ancient art and artifact
The lady must release.
Fine jewelry, mahogany,
A vase of higher merit,
The broken family gathers for
The treasures they inherit.
Like walking dead,
Grave benefactors
Of a grand estate
Will bear her common treasures to
A quick and common fate.

Take Life

I hardly knew the guy next door,
The second man
I've known
To take his life
By his own hand,
To leave a grieving wife
Who never could disclose
The truth she knows.
A grand mistake.
What made them break?
What pushed him to the edge?
They found him in the hedge,
The weapon, contraband,
In the right hand.
A note left on the sink
Could not reveal
What drove him to the brink.
Statistics show
You'll take your life indoors.
Closed in, closed out,
You never know
What someone's life's about.
Take yours, for instants.

That was years ago.
The case was closed.
The widow closed her house.
The neighbors whisper
Secrets unexposed
But to a spouse.

Of Head and Heart

I leave them both alone a lot,
my head and heart.
They never could work hand in hand.
They're not about to start.
They never will see eye to eye.
They serve a different master.
Every time I feel head strong
my heart beats faster.

Logic works, to my surprise,
when words are softly spoken;
Passion flares, to my demise,
when I'm heart broken.
Lusting for the perfect mate,
I always make my move too late.
In and out of love, I put
the horse behind the cart.
Obey my head
or listen to my heart?

On The Porch

The monarch miracle
Is swooning round the bush.
The ever cautious goldfinch
Finally floats from out the tree.
The jeweled siphon
Of invisible wings
Swift as a blink
Suspends to drink.
Slow motor grinding
Lands the bumble bee.

The anxious cat,
Annoyed that
Her hunt is doomed to fail,
Unfurls her tail
And with her porch bound
Steps of silk
Moves toward her warming
Dish of milk.

Now Nancy

Nancy who?
    Only you
    For the rest of my life.

Nancy why?
    I can't fly
    If you aren't my wife.

Nancy what?
    Hits the spot
    Any time, any place.

Nancy where?
    In the air
    In my hair and my face.

Nancy when?
    Now and then
    At a romantic pace.

Nancy how?
    Here and now
    With your heart close to mine
    Beating fast
    Till the last star will shine.

Sanctuary

A tolling of the vespers bell;
The darkness covers me.
The Abby latch is lifted
Like my vow of chastity.
He enters with his taunting chant,
The tempter of my trust.
He whispers through the sepulchers
His ancient prayer of lust.
The swallowing of sacrament,
The pouring of the blood,
The holy face is hidden deep
Beneath the priestly hood.
So weak of flesh, I offer him
My prayer rug from the east,
On which I spread my sacrificial
Flesh before the beast.
With mockery, he enters me.
His great divining rod
Personifies his presence as
My nemesis or god.

In fear I wake, again to break
My tether with the past.
How long will I be prisoner to
The spell that has been cast?
Be merciful to me, I plea.
How long will longing last?

American Farewell

Paint me pink and use me yellow
Pale me sallow cream
Running hot and running shallow
Freezing in the stream

Serve me up hero and harlot
Bloat me over full
Blame me black and scorn me scarlet
Shame me Sitting Bull

Black my eyes but swear you love me
Kiss me till it's true
Ease me in but please don't shove me
Toward red white or blue
Turn my back and cry self pity
Architecture down
Greening of the perfect city
Browning of the town

Lay me out where all can see me
Let me make you cry
Plastic wreath and garland green me
Tell my folks good bye

Love Is

Love breaks the boundary; Love is church *and* king.
Bow humbly down and kiss love's holy ring.
One loving moment, and time falls away.
One loving touch, and all is in it's sway.
Seep, love, into my deepest, darkest place.
Move in my walk and halo round my face.
Flow freely through my bone and flesh and hair.
Extend my heart to sickness and despair.
Burn over me, a flame without disguise.
Blush in my cheeks, and radiate my eyes.
Embrace, sweet love, my spirit and my soul,
My every thought persuade, and act control.
Let no man question that my peace and strength
Rests in your endless height and width and length.
Love liberates when limits are increased.
It blooms when expectations are released.
Love grows with love, reciprocal and free.
Love stays and stays when youth and virtues flee.
And when my bone and flesh and hair *must* go,
Say I *was* love, and your love made it so.

Maple Tree

The queen of Autumn stirs again
Before she falls asleep.
She throws her hair into the air
As winds around her sweep.
Her syrup sap co-mingles
With the gentle touch of frost,
The magic so miraculous
Reality is lost.
The color flowing from her limbs
Cannot be reproduced.
Except as nature dictates
Will the changes be induced.

Crepe paper leaves are snapping
With a delicate release.
They swirl in thousands, whirling
As their multitudes increase.
What jewels are these that with the breeze
Are driven like the rain,
A golden maple shower from
A loftier domain,
Or slowly spin and spiral
With a cadence and an air
That hypnotize when to the skies
We're forced to stop and stare?

They tumble, circus acrobats,
With nonchalance and nerve.
They're brought from nooks.

They're pressed in books
Their beauty to preserve.
Their gold before a conifer
Or bright October sky
Will vibrate light to dazzle even
Leonardo's eye.

The pattern of their carpet
On a verdant forest floor
Will beg you tread a softer step,
To notice them before
Their color yields to nature
And their humus to the earth
To propagate the never ending
Cycle of rebirth.
The showering of her leaf foretells
The coming of the ice.
The maple tree confirms for me
We live in Paradise.

The Last Ride

He leans his head against the wall
Deflated as his basketball,
A certain three point shooter from the past.
Now his games are played in alleys
Where his courage never rallies,
With his speed and resolution fading fast;
But he knows this trip is going to be his last.

Make no plans beyond tomorrow.
Leave your loved ones locked in sorrow.
Breach the limit of your mother's heart and purse.
Make this trip a special journey,
Meet your after life attorney,
Meet the driver and the dealer of your curse
As you crawl into the back seat of your hearse.

Long black limousine unholy
Rolling resolute and slowly
Through this neighborhood gone totally insane,
Drawing children by the masses
From their playgrounds and their classes
While your devil drives the needle to the brain,
And the suicide is coursing through the vein.

Long black limousine, unholy,
Long black limousine, unholy,
Long black limousine roll slowly
Through the reign.

Pine Glen

When seasons are unhurried,
Winter staying long enough
And repeating itself a couple of times
To give all a chance to partake,
When spring and summer and autumn
Are spoken of in terms of "more beautiful",
When friends are made
With promise of remaining so,
When beauty of nature
And warmth of hospitality
Extend an invitation to linger,
Then taking leave
Would be a sad concern,
Could I not feed on
Thoughts of my return,
As toiling birds through summer
Seem to know
Sustaining feeders
Wait for them in snow.

I Want To Be

I want to be beneath the sea
    where fishes swim.
I want to soar where angels roar
    with seraphim.
I want to be an island
    parted from the main,
Forever in my self,
    my heart's domain.

Geography Class

When I was thirteen
A flood consumed me
In Geography class
And Marilyn Geiser
Asked if I was going to faint.
I turned white as ash.
Then I was sent to the medical room.
Then I was sent home.
My poplin jumper was a mess.

Before I ever allowed
His hand beneath my dress
I knew the areas
I wanted him to touch.
I could guide him.
I had been there,
Flooding myself
With hot diffusement
Under clean white sheets.

When love flowed upward
From my feet
And set a fever in my cheeks
And his mouth moved across my neck
I threw my will and future to the wind.

My baby now lies
Cupped upon my breast.
Her breath is sweet and sour.
I draw her to my face
And kiss her wet, warm, parts
Before I swoon back
To the seventh grade
Where war and religion
Sulk on the back row
Of my Geography class.

First Birth

Oh, you and me,
    The stars....eternity.

A gift, a clue,
    In flesh, and with a name.

To live now, and again
    From whence we came.

Born of the stars
    To stars we will ascend

To feel, to love, together
    Without end.

And when again back to
    Our home we soar,

Oh, you and me,
    The stars....forevermore.

Building a Nation

Blaze through the wilderness Lewis and Clark.
Charter the land for a national park.
Statehood Wyoming, a place no one needs.
Bargain Manhattan for trinkets and beads.

Hold off the Spanish till Texas is ours.
Use all the muscle that congress empowers.
Nail down our future and spike down the track.
Steam roll the savages holding us back.

Conquer the plains with the carbine and rail.
Build a state road on the old Chisholm trail.
Form our own Mexico. We'll call it "new".
I'll take Montana, give Utah to you.

Louisiana! The French can't refuse.
We're only wanting what land we can use.
But now we need islands exotic, specific.
Let's make it Hawaiian. They're quite south pacific.

Purchase Alaska from Russia for change.
We're needing more room to sing Home on the Range.
Rest on the seventh and then take a notion
To justify claim to a bordering ocean.

America, you're looking great!
Sail on, sail on, oh ship of state.

Out of Paris

My heart floats back to one grand day
When we drove out to Giverny
With seven strangers in a van
From Paris where our trip began.
At Versailles, Louis and Marie
Were perfect hosts for history,
But kings and palaces gave way
To nobler works at Giverny.

The lily pads, the pond, the bridge,
The hay stacks golden on the ridge,
Vibrant images artistic,
Reconformed impressionistic
In a bold enlightened way
By the hand of Claude Monet.
It was here he sipped his stew
In a yellow room and blue

Trimmed in oriental art,
Food and family but a part
Of the grounds and manse entire.
This was where he fanned the fire
Of genius with paint and brush;
Canvas softer than a hush,
Where chicks and herbs and flowers did grow
About his life and studio.

The images so bold and clear,
As if the artist lingered here,
Like we would linger for reprieve
When our caravan took leave.
With no one but the guard about
We stayed until the lights went out.
How could we ever feel enough
For this estate with Monet's stuff?

We ate our dinner late that night
In quaint Vernon, by candle light,
In love with France and wine and flowers.
Then the train to Saint Lazare
Rocked us to a deeper sleep,
Rich with what our hearts would keep.
There on occasion comes a day
When life spreads light like a Monet.

Dylan

You're like a bike.
You're special alloy steels.
You're light and tight.
You're shiny paint and wheels.
You whistle along
In the wind, like a song.
You're ten speeds, High and Low.
You shift like a Schwin.
When you're ready to win,
You race like a Peugeot.
Your sprockets aligning
In synchronized timing
With little left to chance,
You'll cross the line
In record time,
And win my Tour de' France.

A Card Played

Death caught a trumpless trick
And you were gone.
I caught your desperate glance
When truth came to your chair.
A childlike begging prayer
You sent to me,
An anxious pleading
For a referee.

Your reckless play
Had caught you unaware.
I wish with all my heart
I had a trump
To make you shriek delight
And send you for
Another whiskey,
But I don't.

We will not coffee and dessert tonight,
Nor talk of cards that fell.
We will not love before the fire
When guests are gone.
I walk into the stars.
I see your unbelieving stare.
You were so reckless
When you fell.

There will not be
Another night like this.
There will not be
Another hopeless glance,
Another last, long look
Into the begging eyes.
Death got the lead
And you were out of trumps.

Aging

Not when the fishing boat capsized,
Not when I lost control on the ice on I-95,
Not even when they dragged me
strapped and bleeding from Mount Hood.
Not until
this week in the clinic,
with lab tests in her head,
a Lipitor clipboard
clasped to her sterile smock
when she frowned
"We need to talk"
did I detect
the easy footfall,
the stranger
in the hall.

At Last

It's been a long time coming
But it's going down right
The taste of your love
And it's lasting all night
Like working a puzzle
To get to your bed
But it's here and it's now
And it's gone to my head

When I think of the hours
We waited and wanted
The hours our loving
Can never retrieve
Your touch is more tender
Our lips linger longer
And time is refunded
And I can believe
That forever your vision
Will hold me in grace
Forever your touch
And your kiss
And your face

Fire of the Soul

About the campfire's dying light
Bright faces flush and failing light
Confuses sparks among the trees
With misconceived realities
Like dancing shadows in a cave
Might bring us close to what we crave,
While far away a blinking star
Makes light of how remote we are,
Within ourselves, outside the scope
Of immortality, save hope.

Fire, once our source of light and heat
Now only partial needs must meet.
As we evolved we captured light,
Advancing days into the night,
Reminding us how far we came
In close communion with the flame
As ours diminishes and dies
Without a ray of compromise
Except as hope burns in our soul
Consumptive, far beyond control.

Aurora Borealis

Beyond the atmosphere, when northern nights are clear
Nature spills ionic ink,
Pouring color, bleeding scarlet hues through space
Shot back with spears of
Blue and white
So bright
The stars
Relax.
When swept into this trail of fire and ice
One wonders twice.

Closing Time

The tables are turned.
All the chairs have been moved from the floor.
They're sweeping the shattered relationships
Out the back door.
With animal stalking
And slow whispered talking
The sexual favors are earned.
The couple who left to make love has returned
To find broken timbers
To rebuild the bridges they burned.

The singles all lick
At their wounds of rejection
And howl at the moon
In the old self deception
In the long morning hours
When the ritual court is adjourned,
And truth crawls back home
Like a faithful old hound that returned
To lay at the foot of the bed, unconcerned,
After lessons re-learned,
While they cling to the chance
That tomorrow night's dance
Won't leave them the ones who are spurned,
While ten thousand plastic topped
Broken legged tables are turned.

Sentinel Cedars

Sentinel cedars
March across the
Appalachian foothills
Bivouac on limestone bluffs,
Huddle in their bear like coats against the elements.

Staunch and grounded
Rooted where little else will grow
Claiming space neglected by trees more selective.

Defying green,
Uniformed more toward a rudimentary brown.
Scrub cedars,
Unconcerned with symmetry or proportion.
Overlooked for beauty or decoration.

Accentuating base instincts, to grow
Sometimes two or three trunked.
Bold acceptors
Of wind and snow,

Sanctuaries to birds,
Guardians of a natural beauty,
Reminders of a firmer base.

Solid soldiers,
Faithful to the post.
At ease, trees.

Ecumenical Ox

Lumbering across continents,
Fording oceans, unyoked,
The immaculate beast
Grazed toward the middle east,
Fathered a calf,
Then, re-harnessed,
Dragged slowly into future generations
Until the rough hewn cart
Bogged down in an ocean covered crater
Of an ancient star.

Unable to pull free,
Sinking to his knees,
The bull lay down to die
And there, with one last
Blinking of his weeping eye,
Focused on the future and the past,
Saw a forming constellation blast.

A Chilling Freeze

Skate out with me across the ice
And listen to the silence of the snow
That lies so lightly on the frozen lake.
It wakes and runs
A sentry at the broach
Alarmed
By our approach.

The night's as cold as it is black.
The wind that laid below the levy lifts
The blankets of the season's early snows
And moves as if to turn us back
From danger
Nature
Knows.

We pause to still our pounding pulse,
The crystal cracking of the ice cold stars
Reflected in the frost around our feet
Implores "Go back".
We dare not move.
"Come closer then".
We stay.

Our frosted breath so mingles our concern
That Spring may find us locked in fear this way.

The Rose Room

The light that shines within the room
Reminds them of the afternoons
Of mutual desire
When dreams were
Laid out on an oriental
Carpet by the fire.
The images they scattered on the floor
Were blown away.
The closing of the door,
The back draft of the force
That drew them in,
Propelled them into
What was taught as sin.
But sinning carried forward into love
Beyond the room, the fire, the light above,
Beyond what they would disregard as sin
And back into the room of love again.

Patriotic Pubs

I looked into the face of Ireland more than once.
I saw in pubs how she paid the price
Of peasant sacrifice.
I saw the blood of lost rebellion,
I heard the jackal dog of hunger
Sucking at her throat.
I smelled the bogs agrarian.

Agrarian, we live by what we know.
It takes more than a peat bog to make a country.
We count on time to heal our deepest cuts.
We are the sons and daughters of the land,
And we will be the sons and daughters
Long after this day, too, is past.
May we forever, with the ale and song,
Lift up the voice of the Island soul.

Frankfort, Michigan

I am a town that sidles down
a sand dune to the sea.
I harbor boats and secrets
that are only known to me.
The forest that once folded me
in needles of white pine
went south to build Chicago
so Chicago's partly mine,
as partly mine is any man
who walks my shady streets
or moors his craft or downs a draft
or sleeps between my sheets.
The lake, the sand, the trees, the man,
the rich communion, hand in hand,
that teaches lessons we must learn
as children grow and seasons turn;
this is the stuff that forms my heart,
that turns a tourist's head.
Your legacy will live in me
long after you are dead.

Uniquely Me

In Sunday school I was informed
That I was formed of clay.
Now that I'm old I'm being told
My structure's DNA.
We never know just who we are
Or how we came to be
But I can tell you this for sure,
"I am uniquely me!"
In love with life's evolving form
And all that it entails
I sometimes rail against the storm,
I sometimes bite my nails.
The constant message that I hear
Is "Live in love, and not in fear."
I'm told that God created me.
He gave me life and limb.
It could be just the opposite,
That I created Him.

Man of the Planet

The planet does as the planet wants
No matter what the plan.
To ever extol that he has control
Is the ignorance of man.

What is this beast that stomps about
So tense to wear his spirit out,
Who from the ocean floor did crawl
To shout dominion over all,
While sliding from the mud and slime
Evolves angelically divine;

Who lives in rage while held in grace,
Who hurls his insults in the face
Of God and Satan in their space?
The universe too grand to see
Is shrunk by him to small degree
Then split to fearful energy.

Unrest is marrow in his bone.
He can't leave well enough alone.
He grinds a boulder into sand
To sculpt a rock by his own hand.
The gray soft sponge that forms the frown
Demands he hand these ramblings down
To future beasts, who in their search
Will jerk, and in a palsied lurch
Move closer to the glass to see
What lies beyond eternity,

Not knowing if the shadow cast
Lies in the future or the past
Nor how long will the image last.

In love he suckles mouth to mouth
As poles reverse from north to south,
As creatures roam beneath the seas
That melt and flow before they freeze.
While dreamers die and bodies rot
He tries to grasp what he forgot
Despite what is and what is not,
While time and space have no regard
For soldier, teacher, pope, or bard.

Who fans the flame? Who winds the rope?
What gives him fortitude to grope
Toward heaven with a failing hope?
While half his life he lives in dark
Retiring so to charge the spark
That bares his bite and brays his bark.
Though transformed into life through death
He kicks against the final breath
That promises eternal sight,
Eternal ease, eternal light.

He lives in spirit, mind, and form.
His ego soars beyond the norm,
His life so structured to perform
In fear, in war, in jeopardy,
In conflict with mortality,

In constant struggle with his soul
Of which he has complete control
To relegate the seething mind
To spirit, which will then, in kind,
Relinquish to the body free,
To form the perfect trinity.

And though he does all that he can
To form the special superman,
The planet does as the planet wants
No matter what the plan.

Kassie's Song

Kassie is a dancing charm
That I dangle on my arm
While Mozart and Vivaldi serenade

Floating over hills of dreams
Drifting down the music streams
To sleep, her cool and peaceful
Patch of shade.

Song of Ruth

Soldier father, humble mother,
Born from one last union of their love.
Taught not to care, or unaware
She had a right to be resentful of
The cruel state that unkind fate
Subjects us to, unless we choose to rage,
She thus resigned to spend her time
In servitude, and once the cage
For life is locked, and wound time's clock,
For this task only did she show concern.
Through winters long with waning song,
She sang her children, so that we could learn
To live with empty promises and purse,
To give, and not accept life as a curse.

She walked entranced while others danced
Through life. She knew beyond her humble door
She feign would fly, but stayed to dry
An infant tear, while lesser songbirds soared.
I love her song but still I long
This prison and this circumstance to leave,
To have her know for her I grow
Toward heaven, and for her do I believe.
Her simple laws have been the cause
I could not help this basic law to learn:
"Truth slips disguised into our lives."
I know this law within her soul does burn.
And though not subject to the total truth,
I've heard an excerpt from the song of Ruth.

Nancy In Ireland

I came with Nancy to Ireland,
And Nancy knows leprechauns better than I,
Or better than anyone I'll ever know.
And while we slept nights with the window wide open
The wind sent the spirits to perch on my pillow
And whisper in Gaelic while Nancy did dream.

"We wouldn't be telling you secrets of Ireland
If you hadn't brought her to lie with us here.
Her visit is heaven and we mean to have her
Return when her soul is released to the wind.

But while she is sleeping and while you are not
(and who can say who is entangled in dreams)
We'll visit you nightly and tell you why Ireland
Is more than a mystery, and more than it seems."

So nightly they rode on the wind to our chamber,
And nightly spilled secrets all over our sheets,
And I know they slipped 'neath the covers for Nancy.
I saw her smile in her sleep.

So I'll never come back to Ireland without her,
'Cause they'll never visit if she's not along.
And we can share stories of why Nancy loves us,
And we can love Nancy in dropeen and song.

The Bomb

We lie in Santa Fe about
What lies
Beyond the Rio Grande,
On plateau Pajarito,
On the land
That was a gay boys' ranch
Where Oppenheimer rode
One sunny day
A concept to explode.
Eminent domain,
A compound
Sacred and profane,
The birthing
Ward of mass annihilation
Lost Almost
To current generation.
No longer called Manhattan
And Chicago,
Now Nagasaki, Kandahar,
The Cochiti Pueblo.

In Santa Fe we lie about
Our will to live within
Or live without
The tension born,
The fear we can't conceive.
We rise at dawn
To wait upon
The Atom
And the Eve.

River of Intensity

If I could leave this muddy bank
    for places more intense
I'd float for days with awkward ways
    that didn't make much sense.
I'd wish for healing of sick dogs,
    for windowed cherry pies,
For purple grass and amber trees,
    and cumulous skies;
To drift till my iminotion
    opened to a vaster ocean,
Deeper than pacific rim,
    and that's when I would start to swim.
Oh, river of intensity,
    flow close to my back door.
May no one jealous ask of me,
    "What are you waiting for"?

Mozart at Night

Balanced like a mobile
From a golden quarter moon
The stars intone
The rhythm of the tune.
What shall we do tonight, brain?
What shall we do tonight?
Compose, until the melody is right.
With wine and quill, creating till
We see the early light.

Music through Vienna,
Vibrations for a king,
Sweeter than the angels when they sing.
What shall we do tonight, heart,
Until we fall asleep?
Let's twinkle with the little stars
Out in the deep.
Eine kleine nacht musik,
And then we fall asleep.

With head and heart eternal art
Is conjured in the night
Within creation's narrow band
Bridging dark and light.

Annie B. and Nick

When you grieve, grieve not for her alone.
Grieve for persons who cannot sound grief.
Grieve for lives spent shallow and alone.
Grieve for trees that break before they bend.

Walk back streets with the homeless and the lost.
Grieve for hollow heroes sent to war.
Grieve that they do not embrace the strength
To look into their souls and answer "No".

Take your grief to places that she knew.
Find her in the reverence of the wind.
Yours together is eternal life.
Yours together is eternal love.
Yours is strength to those
Who cannot grieve.

Magical Land

If I'm not mistaken, this ought to be Ireland.
The wind blew me in on a drizzling breeze.
Delivered me daintily down around Dalkey.
Sat me down smooth and as sure as you please.

Now I'll take a bite out of any old rainbow,
And garnish it up with a bit 'o your green,
Wash it down with a pint in your Pub with Pat Riley,
McCormick, O'Shaunessy, Shaw, and McSheen.

Then I'll draw my dropeen in front of a peat fire,
And listen to legends of Leprechaun lore,
Awaiting the wind that will whistle me westward
To Greenfield and Galway and Golam Head shore.

At night I will dream with your dwarfs and your druids
And pray I may live all the rest of my days
Tangled in all of your tricks and you treasures,
Now that I know of your magical ways.

Reconciliation

I've been sleeping alone
With a wound in my heart.
Around midnight I can't bear the pain.
There's no one to touch
But I feel very much
Like I'll maybe start living again.

Not talking to anyone other than me,
I tire of my own lame lament.
Felt the faint cooling breath
Of an angel tonight.
I know that she surely was sent
As a sigh from the woman I'm paining about,
Though she can't understand my despair.
She would rather I cuddle my head on her breast.
She would rather I breathe in her hair.
She would rather I wouldn't divide us like this.
She would rather leave anguish unspoken.
I would rather she just let me know that she knows
What it's like when a heart has been broken.

But I'll conquer my pride
I'll return to her side
With my pieces of heart in my hand,
And I know that she'll take me back into her bed,
And I know that she may understand
Why I can't be alone any more than she can
How our lives are forever as one
With the discord, the turmoil, the parting, the pain,
The mending, the loving, the fun.

Autumn

Come walk with me this evening to the lake
And let the last October colors take
Your breath away.
Always too rushed to wait
They're changing even as we hesitate.
Oh, beauty that can rival even thee
Awaits us on this window shopping spree.

The neon light reflects along the shore
The closing of the season's jewelry store.
Step up with me and take one final glance
At this array of precious radiance
Before the final shuttering is done
To display windows fashioned by the sun.

October wind that mocks your pretty hair
Is stealing jewelry, even as we stare.
So bold a thief….so anxious to confess
By pinning broaches in your hair and dress.
Oh, jealousy, that I could bring forth such
A glow from you, as he does with his touch.

Accomplices to thievery are we.
Come, steal away, and let October be
Our reason for committing such a crime.
Come, let October's bluster fill our mind
And soul with pleasures of this petty theft.
There's so few window shopping seasons left.

Two Surprises

I can't remember when the snow began.
It may have been the other morning when
My cat took sick, about twelve days ago.
I glanced outside and thought, "It's gonna snow".
It started slowly. Clouds began to gather.
(I'm speaking of my cat and not the weather)
Her humor changed. I notice all her fears.
She's been with me for almost thirteen years.
Then it grew heavy. I was worried that
(I'm speaking of the weather, not my cat)
I couldn't make it to her vet in time.
The snow was deep. The roads were closed, and I'm
Not one to cope with changes so intense.
Ameilda died, and in her last defense
I'd have to say she lived and passed on sweetly,
Like me in snow, alone, but not completely.
I know they're always forming in the skies,
But death and snowstorms take me by surprise.

War and Sacrifice

I would not sacrifice my boys to fuel a war.
I've seen them wasted in a foreign land,
Like dry sticks tossed onto a dying fire.
I've heard the praise and accolades
From generals and senators,
And know how pale it washes
Over a mother's face,
Too late and far too insincere.

An army is composed of
Regiments and Companies and Legions,
A family of but one or two.
An army can re-group,
A regiment rebuild.
A family can ill afford the loss.
I would not sacrifice my boys for my land.
Their mother and I could not bear the pain.

Dissipating Grief

He said it wouldn't
when touching hands said
Life will go on.
But it did.

Honey still went into tea.
Bulbs burned out.
Socks went to laundry coupled
And returned divorced.
Grass grew yet.
Monthly bills were met.

Routine flowed slowly
back into the grieving hole
And life went on.

Christmas Child

Never a Christmas morning,
Never a Christmas eve,
That I am not a child again
Eager to believe
In miracles and mysteries
In love, and hope and peace.
Never will I grow so old
That I cannot release
The spirit of the Christmas child
Awakened with good cheer
To wish you love and hope and peace
This year and every year.

Summer at the Lake

Sand dunes into beaches
Lighthouse into fogs
Log flumes into rivers
Marshes into bogs

Blue jeans into tennis shoes
Forests into trails
Brambles into buttercups
Cherries into pails

Sidewalks into storefronts
Nature into hikes
Petoskies into paperweights
Old folks into bikes

Paintings into art fairs
Movies into books
TVs into radios
Songbirds into rooks

Garages into galleries
Yard sales into gold
Discards into treasures
Saving into sold

Attics into antiques
Junk into design
Beachfronts into mansions
Average into fine

Fly rods into rainbows
Mayflies into bait
Walleyes into cattails
Chances into fate

Backdoors into kitchens
Cousins into cooks
Pasta into paper plates
Grills into chinooks

Farmland into orchards
Fruit trees into skies
Blossoms into berries
Berries into pies

Beaches into picnics
Families into fun
Fireworks into holidays
Gliders into sun

Lawnmowers into pushing
Thunder into rain
Screen doors into slamming
Sunburn into pain

Weather into changing
Breezes into gales
Caution into venture
Sailors into sails

Concerts into Thursday nights
Your heart into mine
Sundays into churches
Water into wine

Teasing into touching
Glances into eyes
Passion into longing
Kisses into sighs

Playmates into couples
Evening into night
Couples into drive-ins
Drama into fright.

Photos into albums
Porches into swings
Sunsets into symphonies
Lovers into rings

Grandpas into poets
Poems into themes
Grandmas into memories
Children into dreams

Birches into bonfires
Rivers into bays
Love songs into lullaby's
Sailboats into quays

Marvel into milky way
Wishes into stars
Wonder into northern lights
Fireflies into jars

Diamonds into rhinestones
Silver into tin
Each summer into Michigan again

Autobiographically Less Than One Hundred Words

My mom named me Tom
View me as a moving mist
That may or may not exist
Belting out the same old tune
Howling naked at the moon
Just like two men out of three
Not up to capacity
Selling out to make a buck
Sports car or a pick up truck
Cursing any senseless war
Questioning what love is for
Wrestling with the over soul
Scoffing civil self control
Difficult to reason with
Moving just outside the myth
Born beyond restraints of time
Reaching for the perfect rhyme
Chances lost but wisdom found
Practice for next time around

Let Your Heart Lead the Way

If you love a girl but don't know what to say,
Let your heart lead the way.
If her's is the beauty that dazzles your eye,
Don't let the chance pass you by.
Don't listen to logic or reason.
Go right to the flirting and teasing.
This is the moment you hold in your sway.
Let your heart lead the way.

You might send her flowers,
Or candy, or verses,
But not to pursue her is wrong,
And what's worse is,
Someone may steal her.
Then what would you say.
You will just sigh, as your dream fades away.
Don't let her go.
Give her reason to stay.
Let your heart lead the way.

And when you have won her,
With all of her charms.
A lifetime of love
You will hold in your arms.
As your future unfolds like a romantic play
You will recall how you didn't delay
To capture the moment
On one special day
When you let your heart lead the way.

I See You on the Fourth of July

I see you on the fourth of July.
I'm in the crowd that you are marching by,
Estranged as any member of the band.
You're fireworks that I can't hold in my hand.
You're stars and stripes and the rockets' red glare,
Exposing the faces of people who stare
At your innocent beauty exploding this day
In darkness around us, then falling away
To a vision remaining within the mind's eye
When we're old and alone on the fifth of July.

Fifty Years and Less

Fifty years old he was this week.
"But he doesn't look fifty," they said.
"He wears his age well," they were heard to say.
Maybe he does, and maybe it's because
He is not angry enough.
He lacks emotion,
Not enough argument.

A man his age should rant and rave.
He should spawn controversy,
Else he is dangerous,
Like a mad dog in the street.
Citizens will lock their doors and look at him
Wide eyed, through finger spread venetian blinds
Till someone sure can be summoned to shoot him.

A man who slowly turns the corner
Of a half century,
Looking left and right too many times
Before he steps from the curb
Is a man to breed caution.
He will most likely have a fever in his groin
And a purse too fat with someone else's coin,
Or too firm a position in the church,
Or too tight an arm clutch with a politician.
He is a lantern ready to be overturned
In some O'Grady's barn.

Fraternize with a fifty year old man
Only if he snaps and snares
And shows his teeth,
Or coughs up phlegm
From too much ale,
Or smells, sometimes, of urine.
It's too late to be cautious at fifty.

As Catbirds Do

A catbird faltered in the rain and fell.
He fought for life
But death salted his tail.
The cold, thick rain
That touches birds too deep
Now draped with pearls
Two fragile wings, asleep,
As if to ease the guilt
For letting death
Come close enough
To steal a catbird's breath.

A fallen bird
Left dead out in the rain.
Or maybe it was just a heavy dew.
Or maybe it was just a heavy do.
Or maybe it was just a heavy due.

Missing You

The summer fragrance of your negligee
Floats on the pillow where you used to lay.
We had a quarrel and you turned away,
And since that time my skies have turned to gray.

Last night I went walking where we used to walk,
And the only thing missing was you.
The moon and the stars, they were in the right place,
But they wondered, like I wonder too.
How could you leave when our love was a vow,
A promise for us to fulfill.
The moon and the stars, they may burn just as bright,
But the light in my life never will.
Won't you come back and tell me that things will be right?
Won't you please let us have one more try?
Can't we make ours a love that's as fixed and as bright
As the moon and the stars in the sky?

Community Porch

Our porch is an extension of our home
To which a visitor may come
To bear good news
Or share a drink and food
To which no ill can come
But only good.

Inviting music, candles,
Birds or squirrels
Or boys and girls,
Or butterflies
Round checkered tablecloths,
Or lamps at evening
Visited by moths.

The music of our living village sings
Across the wicker rockers and the swings
While poetry is taught and learned
Exciting secrets caught and turned
To midnight whispers
When the neighbors sleep
And moonbeams sweep
Across the floor
Into my window
And beneath my door
And I am drawn onto the porch at night
To holy silence, and celestial light.

When You're Away

Time jumps the tracks
When you're away,
My schedule swinging
On a stubborn hinge.
The fragrance of the kitchen's gone,
With Folgers on a binge.
The bed is boring,
Linens not as crisp.
Someone sleepless,
Someone sorely missed.

Our garden doesn't seem to shine.
The colors took a holiday.
Our home is in a serious decline.
Our swing, our chairs,
They have no interplay.
All things yours and mine
Are idly on display.

I spin about the town
Without my gyroscope,
My hands and schedule free,
Make vain commitments
To our coupled friends,
Not hearing who I want to hear,
Not seeing who I want to see,
Feeling colder on one side
Till you return
The other half of me.

Dreams Kilarney

The wind blew Kilarney around
The first night I was in Ireland,
And leaning from my window at midnight
The clouds raced by the stars
And the stars winked
Of Yeats and leprechauns, and Synge.

Oh, this is the land of sensation.
This is a pallet for poets,
An island endowed with a spirit and soul.

The stars and the wind
Let the secret slip forth.
Take up your walking stick
Out through the gate.
County Kerry will whisper
To those who will hear.

Death of a Young Boy

After the initial shock
I smiled on hearing he had died.
Without remorse,
I accepted what was told me.
Beautiful in life….a joy,
Delicate as a taste,
Not ruined by gluttony.

As a lost night traveler
Might catch a glimpse of light
In a deep forest
To re-ignite his hope,
So my soul quickened at the news,
And only then did I comprehend
The worth of his short life.

Like a newly lighted candle,
Pinched early,
Then carried from the hearth
To a remote area of the home
Where light is more dear,
His death made sense to me,
As did his life.
For me, who has burned too long,
The news was not sad.

Crow

I've seen a tree explode with birds
Touched off on a winter day
Like someone pushed the plunger
On a charge of dynamite
To send black powder skyward.

Late in the day,
When gray both earth and sky
And nothing save the wind moves,
A black endless ribbon
Has dipped and swirled
Across the horizon,
Purposeless, it seems, in destination.

But you, lone bird,
Black against the day,
And motionless of wing,
Slice through the fog
As though driven by purpose
To glide onto a dead world,
Drawn, spellbound, from a safer perch,
Into this cold and fog-locked afternoon.

Then from afar, a cry,
And the ocean of fog breaks
With the beat of your ebony oars
And you respond to your lost companion
And disappear into the drowning sea.
Take me. Take me. Take me.

Beneath The Veil

A veil of gossamer she wore
From seraphim endowed.
It draped about her chastity,
protective as a cloud.
I saw beneath the veil but once,
her innocence entire;
such beauty as to fan the carnal
flames of my desire.

Past Paradise

They lost the guise of paradise
To a seductive song,
When beauty blew and billows grew
Before a breeze so strong
They scarce could hear the songbird in the glade.
The clouds suppressed the sun, and in the shade,
Beset by all the beauty they had started,
He languored, unaware that she had parted.

How sad his soul, how sobering the day
He realized that she had been away.
Now all the future they had vowed to share
Could not return the garden to repair,
Nor propagate the passion and the pride
She planted, when she chose to be his bride.

How long a lie, lame alibi,
That blushes like the promise of a rose,
Can stay concealed, rest unrevealed,
Till time elects the manner to expose,
Through bits of light, in darkest night,
Vague recall of a truth already known
To one sad heart, whose only part
Was disregarding rumors that had grown.

And though the garden persevered,
In spite of the neglect,
As from a dream, it didn't seem
So sweet in retrospect.
The fragrance of the flora, the
Intoxicating sky
That held them close in love's repose
As strangers wandered by,
Would never be the same to him,
Nor sacred their affair
As it was then….as it was when
He thought that she was there.

Balance

With war cries hurled around the world,
With fear invading dreams,
We long for tolerance and peace,
The balance of extremes.
That balance lives within The Birth
Two thousand years ago.
The love and light that on that night
Began to flame and grow
Still lives within our hearts today,
Still holds us in it's grace.
When we force out the fear and doubt
His love will fill the space.
Our nation knows, through lost heroes,
What sacrifice entails.
We'll make their loss a worldly cause
To see that love prevails.
In times like these, when miseries
Plague nation, life, and home,
Just take the Christ Child to your heart
And make His love your own.

Vernal Equinox

Winter came again and found me
    In my same repose
And now the fields are melting down
    More quickly than they rose.
The meadow in the flowering stage
    Will call me from my hearth
And I will rise and roam the land
    Kinsman with the earth.
What calls me from my shelter deep?
    The ermine and the fox,
Along with me, acknowledge thee,
    The vernal equinox.

Hitting the Road

I certainly would like to keep
My Harley cycle and my Jeep
And though it may sound sexist
That's where she wants to park her Lexus.
Right where my shiny hog and CJ-7
Have been since June of 1967.
Her four wheel drive and anti-lock
And undercoat are all a crock,
Just like the sacra-cranial massage
She gets from Bruce Masseuse
And his entourage.

I'm gonna fix my wheels some day
And maybe ride them both away.
Then she'll be sorry she was fast
In trading future for the past,
Cause then she'll have to live
With that big sissy,
Her Lexus and his Mitsubishi.

Just a Little Girl and Me

Many are the times I've seen her
Up into his lap go scrambling,
Cuddle close with eager eyes
And through his story land go rambling.
Down a river he would take her,
Often save her from a storm.
She with eyes aglow, would listen,
Moving closer, keeping warm.
For she saw the storm was restless,
And would soon without a care.
Lift her from the safe protection
Of her grandpa's easy chair.
So, upon request, he often
Had to alter force of gale
If he cared to have his colleague
Finish listening to his tale.

Or, they'd journey to a mountain,
Where upon a bear they'd stray.
She would have it be a "good" bear,
Leaving him without a say.
Times when she would brew the coffee
Just the way that he was wishing
Or have the cabin neat and clean
When he came home from mountain fishing.
Times when they would roam together
Through the berries on the hill;
This is when she loved the stories,
When they hearkened to her will.

So he'd sit and spin a story
And she'd listen with delight
Till a day of playful labor
Tiptoed softly into night.

Story land, I say, and yet
It was a land to them as real
As the one that I am living,
Where my feet cannot be still;
Still enough to take a minute
From the recklessness of day
Just to sit and dream a story
That would take me far away
To a mountain or a river
Where my blackened thoughts would flee
And I'd find my soul's contentment…
Just a little girl and me.

October

Divorce and free me from this sweaty slut
Who, with her warmth, my leaving has delayed.
Awake and wean me on a cooler breeze.
Relieved am I to have this romance fade.
Let die this nagging Summer escapade.

I know that Spring was once my lover too.
I know of Winter's way with older men.
October, now, with melancholy kiss
Reminds me where my love has always been.
I'm ready now to lie with her again.

And when she leaves, I'll contemplate once more
Some forty years of these fast love affairs;
How seasons lie with me and seasons leave
By slipping down my rickety back stairs,
How all these covert meetings will be missed
When time allows one final season's flair.

Retirement

Out a long busy pier
With his new fishing gear,
A bucket of bait,
And a Falls City beer,
A worked-out Chicago machine
With a notion
Retirement invited
To fish in her ocean.
The click of the drag,
The cast of the bait,
A vacuum of future
To kick back and wait
For a mermaid.

The mobile home vacant,
The silver scales found
On the pier the next morning
Consider him drowned.
He swims past the Social Security reef
Garland in seaweed.
His life was as brief
As a strike at a lure.
Now the pull of the tide
Draws him under to chambers
Where he will reside.

And the bait casting rig
That he worked to afford
Will be sold by his widow,
But still the last word

Will be sung by the mermaid
Of Aqua and Foam,
As the salt air eats into
The fishing reel chrome,
While his love swims him back
To his primeval home.

My Blue Canoe

The maple leaves
    in legions
    are damned against
    my casts.
Every other effort
    is naught.
The feathered hook,
    with amber grace,
    lands lightly
    on the face of autumn.
The surface opens
    and heaven
    shines up to me
    as blue as my canoe.

Photographs

I'm six years old.
I'm thirty three.
She's sipping coffee
Or high tea.
They don't resemble
Her or me
As we are now
Or soon will be.

A local businessman
Took these.
It's somewhere in
The Pyrenees.
This is her mom.
This is my dad.
This is the winter
When we had
The snowstorm of
The century.
This is her favorite
Shot of me.

Here's Jimmy Dale
The week before he died.
That's what's her name,
His girlfriend,
By his side.

Here's one of us
In southern France.

This is that dark
Flamenco dancer
Tiptoeing
To castanets.
That's just as happy
As it gets.

We snapped this in
A photo booth.
These are her cousins,
Jane and Ruth.
That's our first home.
That's Tom and Jim.
He's crying cause
We scolded him.

These are my parents
On their wedding day.
This is the cottage
Where we used to stay
Those summers out on
Crystal Lake.
How many photos
Did we take?

Five thousand of
A hundred lives.
We loose them, but
If one survives
To spark a memory
Of the past

How long will our
Short visit last?

We can't remember
That girl's name,
Or when she left,
Or when she came.

Through frozen smiles
The future laughs
At cracked and crumbling
Photographs.

The Periwinkle Prayer

Oh, God, who grants us more than we deserve.
Grace now this place and bounty that is ours.
May lives of those that seem less fortunate
Be blessed with holy fragrance of your flowers,
Our gardens flourish and our paths begin
To follow Him of love and light…Amen

Love

There can be no boundaries for my love,
No mountains or rivers so wide.
If I wanted to say how I love you
I would have to discard all the pride
That so silently steals deep within me
To imprison sweet words in my heart
And soon for the want of expression
Only lies from my lips let depart.

Then I'd try to express in a few empty words
All the love that I want you to know.
I would tell of a love that's as strong as the sea
And as pure as the first winter's snow.
But you'd take these words lightly,
You'd think me a fool
To be carried away by my heart.
Still, my love can't be altered,
But deepens and grows,
As you turn from my glance and depart.

Former Wife

She makes an honest effort at the truth,
Bees of business buzzing round her head.
And only music's therapeutic sleuth
Can resurrect the dead.
Her reason lies in formulas
Too rigid to respect,
While I rebuild the footings
Of the castle that she wrecked.

April

Spring comes in with April
And the warm promise of
Sunshine in her smile
Reaches to the chilling corners
Of my concerns.

I feel within her presence
A pure beginning
And a strong desire to linger.
But her short stay lends merit
To the value of brevity.

She leads us into summer warmth
And we too easily forget her
Except when harsh winds touch us
And we realize
It's colder when she's gone.

Inconstant Heart

When I am overtired
Of what I thought I loved,
The one I live with ired
By my attention proved
Inconstant as before
I seek another chore.

My loyalties fall always short
In labors I attempt to love.
She doesn't know that I consort
With powers below me and above
Before my fickle heart inclines
To grander callings more divine.
It's plain I can't be true to all
Without a monumental fall.

After Life

Try not to cry when I die
Nor dwell on what I did or left undone.
But from the dirge of death turn happily.
Do not remember me or think thoughts of,
Except as I bring to your bed
Redeeming dreams of love.

A Public House

They're not very busy in Ireland
And that's what I like.
Industrial gearing gives way to a stout
And they sing in the pubs of their island.
I want to be party to that sort of spirit.
I want to escape as a cog in a wheel,
To better myself with a pint and a poem.
I want to be Irish a few days a year.

Eternity

I penetrated deep into the starry skies tonight,
Emerging in a halo of celestial light.
Suspended by a single thought as
Vast and undefined as space,
I drifted weightless as a veil
Of long decaying lace.

A votive candle flickered for my sake.
The evening shade was drawn. Beads
Of bone slipped over knuckles like
A snake, escaping from
The dawn.

My empty vessel shatters to the earth.
My ageless spirit flees
Into the aura of rebirth
Beyond the realm
Of Hesperides.

A blinding light divides the universe
Before me as I move. Florescent
Rays of time and space,
All knowledge and all love
Enfold me into spheres
Of life, below me
And above.

Fading Dreams

Geometry more perfect than the egg
contains the dream more
magic than the mist.
Reality that cracks the shell
will not allow extension
to exist.
Fleet is the dream that slips away,
but memory persists.

Road to Success

The road to success is the roughest road
That any man can choose,
With it's trials and tribulations
And the wearing on the shoes,
But the road that leads you straight to hell
Is the road that cowards take,
Where the bumps and ditches
Have all been smoothed,
And the mud is chocolate cake.
So it's up to the man and his conscience
To choose the road that he will.
The rugged one leads to heaven,
But the easy one leads to hell.

Oh, it's a long, hard road and the detour signs
Are temptation along the way,
And it takes a man of spiritual strength
To continue day by day.
So ask yourself which road you are on
And see if it's rough up ahead.
The reward you receive for the life you have lived
Doesn't come until after you're dead.

Angel's Song

The full moon tipped and spilled
Her golden radiance tonight,
So I went out and filled
My magic inkwell with the light.
A virgin quill I fashioned from
The feather of a wing
Of a cherub who impassioned me
To form him words to sing.

I penned with inspiration, music,
More than just a song;
A message that would resonate
Above our earth bound throng.
He sings it now in glorious rhyme,
Our sweet angelic tune,
Outside the known restraints of time,
Beyond our golden moon.

Winter Wore This Year

Winter wore this year my patience out,
Testing what the season is about.
White whirling woods with black bark inter spaced
Drowning deep in darkling dreams
Woven through the evergreens
Crocheted white and Belgium laced
About a single tree, a single thought
A single message barely caught
Echoes how my lonely life is graced.

Your Beauty

You crippled me when first we met.
Your beauty bruised my eye.
Now handicapped, yours is the mark
I gauge all beauty by.
Soft spring and golden autumn,
Bold summer, green and blue,
Demean my mind, as color blind,
My vision conjures you.

The blush that flows into your cheek,
Your brow, raised in surprise,
The twitching corner of your mouth,
The squinting of your eyes,
The pursing of your eager lips,
The light upon your hair,
This is the beauty I hold up
When beauty I compare.

Do Not Despair

Do not despair when I lie down.
For everlasting love, live on.
For early though my life I leave,
Forever I am gone.
That which we shared
In you will live.
And so your life shall be
Forever draped in memories
Of what was you and me.

Compromise

If ever you were not in my desire
I'd burn a lesser fire,
Or I not in your naked thought,
Then all is naught.
If I hate how you hate a storm
If you hate how I grumble in my cup
Then we can only compromise the norm
Or give it up.

The Lady

The lady reads a lot of books
And hangs her ideas on skyhooks
Too often making matters seem confused.
And in her eagerness to live
Looks over ways that she could give
Her loveliness, for fear of being used.

Between the covers of her book
She's swayed to be more than a cook.
Her life is challenged by a greater cause.
Between the covers of her bed,
Caught up in all that she has read,
She loves in fear of early menopause.

The lady lies about her place
In life, to keep from loosing face.
She smiles through days with her desires unknown.
But she lies best in bed with me
When both of us, completely free
Can touch and taste and laugh and love, alone.

Heroes

So on to greater battlefields
Of glory we could run,
And never stop to ask
If we have done what should be done.
But my breath is getting shorter,
And my muscles feel more tense.
I can't straighten out my reasoning.
My mind is barbed wire fence.
I'm entangled in this maze
Between the enemy and us,
And I can't do anything
To help our cause
But scream and cuss.

Why should we be called the heroes
Just to wear a copper cross,
When the heights of all our gains
Can't match the depths
Of all their loss?
How in hell did anyone like you and I
Get in this mess,
When the whole affair got started
By somebody's second guess?
How in hell did we get chosen?
Did we ask for this command?
I'll be damned if I can see it,
While we all will be God-damned.

Forever Together

I called up my mother in a dream the other night.
I told her I gave up her trinkets.
She said, "That's all right."
It was a clothespin, a handkerchief, and a spoon
That I let go.
But I knew when I did
That she would have it so.

What can we gain when we build
With a thread or a ribbon?
A memories' nest?
Better we have the bird of emotion
On the wing,
Free to fly.

I see a mother bend to kiss her son.
I pick a berry from a bush.
I smell a loaf of bread.
I wear a flannel shirt
That once we shared.
My mother lives with me
In sweet tranquility.

Fifteen Years

Only you know and I know
The source of our love
And can chart for tomorrow
The course of our love:
And the star that direction
Does give to our bark
May explode through the heavens
In foreboding arc.
Yet the strength of our union
Lies not in a star
But in knowing, through crises,
We've traveled this far.
May tomorrow our voyage
Even more pleasant be
With the faith that your love
Finds new strength within me.

Near Your Bed

Find me floating
Near your bed
When you're not here
And then instead
Of thinking of me
Draw me to your heart.
Make me a part
Of your dreams,
And as love seems
To help you fall asleep,
Hold me deep.

How Sad Her Death

She huddles by death's hillock
Near the cemetery gate,
Her haven from hostility and hate.
Her grave concern, she didn't learn
To turn her life around.
With maddened eyes and contrite sighs
She grovels on the ground.
The haunting hemlock hangs his hoary head
In humble homage to her holy bed.
She wildly wonders what her fate might be
If life had compromised
Just one degree.

The hemlock leans to whisper "soon",
The crying clouds, the moaning moon,
The weeping wind, the grieving grass,
The silent soil will hold her fast.

How hated is the hand that holds
The heavy hangman's noose.
How pitiful her pious prayer
That kept her on the loose.
Her ward will find her, by her hand,
Inside her shallow grave.
How loud the toll, how sad the soul
She sought in vain to save.
Man is the fool who yields the tool
To chide her for her sin.
We shut her out,
But nature draws her in.

Orbit

It's not a night and then a day.
The orb on which we ride
But turns away
To turn again,
To spin
Closer to the flame,
A universal moth that came
From universal darkness
Into light,
That knows the day
Because it knows
The night.

Religious Air

Religious air,
In silent prayer,
You closed your eyes to stare
More deeply into space.
You sat in grace.
A smile slid from your face.
Had you sensed the angels near?
Did you fear
Their grave intrusion?
Was the fusion
Of your mind and soul
Beyond control?
What fears of sin
Were sweeping in
On angel wings?
What banal strings
Were knotted into slings?
What magic made it start
To draw you from the real
To heal your heart?
What power in wine and bread
Could turn your head?
I watched the ticking of your eye.
I heard you sigh.
A furrow formed across your brow.
You were not present now.
Your fingers traveled north and south,
Up to your mouth,
As if to stifle fear.
Was God too near?

Did your life of wrong and right,
Of black and white,
Give way to gray?
Did it startle you to find
That prayer was not of mind,
But of the spirit?
Did you fear it?
Did you hear it
When the organ played amen?
Could you come back again?
Or did angels hold you fast,
To look back on your past?

When the prayer ended,
You, suspended
With the angels in the height
Looked back on lives
You left behind,
Locked in the mind.
Locked in the
Fear of dying,
Never flying,
Never trying
To retrieve
A lost belief.
You and the
Angels overhead
Grew radiant in gray,
As your garments fell away.
A voyeur in God's house,
I watched you pray
As you shed your puritanic negligee.

Tunnel of Love

I've been through the tunnel
So many times I've become it.
And through the compression
Of lines of strained rhymes
I can hum it.
The song in my head
Is the song in my heart.
My soul wonders where
It allowed them to part.
And the music that resonates
Now through my bones
Is the hum of the soul
Which is never alone.

Day After Day

The curtains lift
With the shift
Of morning breezes.
Dawn eases
Ore the lawn.

I yawn.
I wake.

My senses take
An inventory
Of each part,
My head, my heart,
The first, the second story,
The spiral stairs,
My pubic hairs,
My skin, my touch,
The French, the Dutch.
The fabric
And the frame
The same
As yesterday
Or Saturday,
Or history,
Or June.
The tune,
The words
I've heard
I hear again,
The spin

Incessant and distinct,
The urge
A dirge
That leads me to the brink.

I pause before my sink.

I rise as Jason rose
That day in Greece
To steal the fleece.
As Caesar took his cup,
I lift mine up.
Jump start
My heart.

I step into the shower.

In time
Replace
The grace
That should be mine;
Maybe this hour.
Re-ignite the flame
My name
Inspired.
I am shameful
Of my image.
I am tired.

How many spins
Are in
The turning

Of this ball,
Before the call,
The fall
Of countless angels
Singing,
Ringing
The demise
Of shape and size,
Before the breaking
Of the bend,
Before the end
Of all pretend?

How many mornings
Will we spend
In glory?
How many chapters
To the story?
How many moons
And tides and tunes?
How many couples
On the arc
Before the dark
Descends?

I brush my teeth,
I shave,
And my life ends.

The Light Within

Before I knew the light without,
    I sensed the light within,
    that grew, and through a darkling doubt,
    my life began to spin
About another DNA,
    her fiber and her fluid,
    till I uniquely turned my way
    to manage as I could
Without the choking cord of life,
    without my mother's milk.
    I fancied girls, I took a wife,
    I fancied jewels and silk.
Then love and I, we struck a spark
    of fiber, blood, and bone,
    that soon emerged from damp and dark,
    one with us, yet alone.
Birth and rebirth, we walk the earth
    anticipating when
    we will ignite the perfect light
    that first we sensed within.

To Build a Wall

I build with callused hands
As gardening demands
A wall of native stones
With aches and groans.
I hesitate
But then create
A wall of rocks
For flags and phlox
To penetrate and overrun
Through rain and sun
And bind with roots
And springly shoots
Till boulders shout
And move about
And tumble down
Go underground
And in their fall
Desert the wall
And leave the plants
To stomp and dance
About the yard
In disregard
Of structure tighter
Or soil lighter
Than the sand
In which they stand.
A foolish chore.
I'll try no more
To stay the spread
Of any flower bed.

Vacation

When to the call of a cloud 'ore a key
    we awake to a gulf breeze blowing,
We shake out our sail to a southerly sun
    while we celebrate, knowing
That soon we will catch in the curl of our sail
    a soft sea wind, slowing.

Come cast your anchor in Coquina Cove
    and slow to the pleasure of shelling.
Stroll down the beaches of sea grass and pine
    and of salty air smelling
Of rain and of mystery, as life washes in
    with secrets compelling.

Sleep in the sand with your hand in the hand
    of your love while the mermaids are singing.
Let your soul swim with them down to dark dungeons
    where eons are ringing,
Sensing in creation's cradle of life
    eternity winging.

With seagulls and pipers walk out in the surf
    as the sun bounces breaker to breaker
And willingly slips to the edge of the earth
    to let the sea take her.
A pelican passes as ancient as light
    that soon will forsake her.

Come to this island whenever you're wanting
    to capture a vagabond feeling.
Come when you know that your ship is in irons
    and you need to be stealing
These breezes that blow with their bandages borne
    in missions of healing.

My Legacy

A stranger to the knowledge of more educated men
My father's class was in our home where poetry began.

> *The fateful valley of the light brigade,*
> *Where formed the face upon the bar room floor,*
> *Love's blinded anger of the highwayman.*
> *Oh, breaking wave that crashes to the shore,*
> *Where tracked the footprints in the sands of time.*

It mingles, what was real and what was rhyme.
The life my cautious father chose
Was epic verse and simple prose.

His constant care, his nagging fear,
His poetry and bottled beer,
His undershirt and pork pie hat,
His wing tipped shoes and all of that
Which made him more than all his parts,
An easy touch for bleeding hearts.
He kept me, in his awkward way,
Protected every waking day
Against the pain he knew would come,
And did, and I was on my own,
Supported by the classic verse
He emptied from his frugal purse.
How beautiful that I can be
A child of his, and poetry.

Nancy's Birthday

There never was in all my life
A girl as sweet as Nancy Lee:
My friend, my critic, and my wife.
How lucky can a booger be?
You stole my heart at seventeen.
You've kept it since that time.
And I can't get it back. You know
I'd sell it for a dime.
So I'm content as years pass by
And you light up a room
To know the light is partly mine.
You are the one to whom
I trust my light; I trust my heart;
I trust my life entire.
You are the one year after year
Who lifts my spirit higher.
So as our birthdays roll around
And you grow old with me,
I'll be the candles on your cake.
I love you, Nancy Lee.

Approaching the Storm

A fog engulfs the bay.
High, away,
thunder tiptoes in.
Heaven's floorboard squeaks.
Then Vulcan speaks,
disturbing secrets of the night.
Electric light
illuminates the air.
I disengage from dreams.
I stare
into the blinking image of my room.
Muted flashes understate the gloom.

I struggle from my sheet
into the heat.
I lift the curtain.
With uncertain
sight I seek
a brighter darkness than I've known.
I hear a foghorn moan.
I'm not alone.

"What is it Tom?"
she whispers, reticent to speak.
The lightening shows the pallor on her cheek,
the shape of bones beneath her gown.
Rain start falling down.
"It's just the starting of the rain,"
I answer as she turns in pain.

"What is it, Tom?"
she murmurs through her sleep.
"It's just the rain,"
I answer, and in pain
she floats back to the deep life atrophy
while reaching out to me.

I stroke her brittle wrist.
Her fingers twist
around my hand.
"Stand close to me,"
she whispers through the dark.
The heavens answer with a stark
reality, and I can see
the dark depravity
of hope upon her face.
Our pulses race
together
as we brace
before the weather
that lifts the heat,
but still denies relief.

Death is a thief,
immune to form,
riding on the storm.

Raven

Fleet acrobat of trapeze art
With cleverness exceeding smart
Your playful act is grand disguise
For fire that burns beneath your eyes.
Black silhouette against the snow
Is allegory we can't know.
Your mystery form of ebony
Says all you need to say to me.
Endowed with magic tongue and beak
If it would gain you, you might speak,
As speak you may to creatures kin
Regarding man's regretful sin;
The endless urge to regulate
That which he can't domesticate.
I see you better than did he.
You can't be trapped eternally.
Your secret's too great to succumb
To perfumed couch of opium.
Fly free, survey your perch below
Where nevermore you pine with Poe.
Grand raven, lord of all outdoors,
The wind, the rain, the skies are yours.
Escape, great bird, from man's domain;
Fly higher than his laws can claim.
Forevermore your spirit grow
As regal chieftain of the crow.

National Ways

Nature loves a bare assed naked man.
Snakes are happy sleeping under rocks.
I like to sleep with England's wife
While England hunts the fox.

Everybody's moving to the suburbs.
Pushers are the keepers of New York.
McDonalds sold a billion burgers.
All were beef and none were pork.

Charles Atlas would never kick sand in your face.
Orson Wells wouldn't go on a diet.
Your wife's little pinkie is in the right place,
And dessert is so yumm…you should try it.

Don't open up a can of worms.
Don't puncture it or pry it.
Who slipped the hormone to little Babe Ruth?
Why won't Cassius Clay Ali buy it?

Kassie Lee

You're a bird and a bee,
And you frequent my tree
With your sweetness and your sound.
You're as light on the air
As the wind through your hair
When you turn my head around.
You can sting like a pin
When the mood that you're in
Is "Don't see me now. I just woke up".
But then you're both my doughnut
And the coffee in my cup.

Insight

When I think I discern
A disguise in your voice
And I feel that your heart isn't true
I will look through
Your stained glass windows
To see who's kidding who.
The eyes are the windows
That see to the soul
And a lover like me
Can peek through.

Love's Return Home

Crystal stars are falling
Down a Hiawathan sky,
Enticing summer lovers,
Trying not to say goodbye,
Beneath the blowing birches,
With beach fires flying bright
In the universal darkness
Of the dancing northern lights
That danced for pristine lovers
On this pristine northern shore
When we were young and into love
Like no one loved before:
When we tried not to say good-bye
For fear we would forsake
The bond that held us like the bond
That locks the land and lake.
How could we know the convoluted
Journey we would take.

That ancient light that fixed that night
Our promise to a star
Has been the light to draw us home
To this Arcadian bar.
Our tattered sails are trimmed from winds
That kept us from our course.
We're back within this haven
With a love we can't divorce.

The stars that fell, the lights that danced,
The fires upon the beach,
Are falling, dancing, burning still;
We're married each to each.
They never left, nor did we leave.
Our union now is sure.
In harmony with nature,
Completed is the tour.
Renewed are vows
We made that night.
In love we lie secure.

The Snake is an "S"

The snake has
A singular style.
He slinks and slithers
Into secret spots.
He slides through swamps.
He sees through slits
He scarcely stirs.
He soaks up sun.
He senses with his tongue
His silver scales do shine.
He savors mice.
He scares us with his hiss.
He doesn't know
He doesn't care
That in our sense
We see him as an "S"

Twenty Years

After years number twenty
And friends number few
After you've placed me first
As I've always placed you,
Can we find the deep pleasure
Of sharing a life
In an outdated custom
Of husband and wife.

Our progression through passion,
Through mind, to the soul,
To the rhythm of family,
Of fixtures, of gold,
Is a dance seldom practiced
By many, for long,
Till the partner is changed
With the turn of the song.

Through an era when oneness
Wins favor with most,
Where the need to share life
With a loved one is lost,
Will we honor, in love,
"Until death do us part".
Let time sound sincerity's
Depth in our heart.

Cats of Peace

Cry hallelujah
        and let lie the cats of peace,
Blue collared, with a bell,
Contented, couched, and creamed,
The only litter in their life
Fresh stepped.

No mascot this
        of General Dynamics,
No colleague of the bull and bear,
No white house pet,

But one, that with
        a gentle stroke
Would noonday nap
Along a Baghdad boulevard.
No fear or false anticipation.
Only feline friendly syncopation.

Andrew's Visit

He came, a "Winter Shaker",
seeking shelter, to our door.
We gladly took him in for
winter's work this year was more
than I had counted on with young
Tom gone away to school.
And each succeeding winter seemed
to caution me, more cruel,
that age, and not the task, made
chopping fire wood seem less fun.
So I was glad to job this chore
to him at twenty one.

I had not seem him since a child,
when on a restless bent,
my brother took his family to
the mountains. Argument
would not return him, but his son
came back to stay a while,
and I could see, occasionally,
my brother in his smile.
Just as I see, Tom took from me
an easy attitude,
I see that Andy took from him
a wild and restless mood.

Andrew liked Jim, our younger son,
and was at ease, in truth,
with something that he saw in him.....
his own, but dying youth:

as when in backward glance we see
a place along the road
we wish that we had stopped to rest
our body and our load,
but caught up in the pace, move on,
pretending there will be
another respite, offering
such cordiality.

Our ways were somewhat strange to him.
His ways were strange to us.
And work he would, just till he could
persuade me to discuss
some deeper topic than an ax,
like good pine needle tea,
or moss, or birds, or stars, or friends,
or immorality.
And I admit that I am weak
to talk of things like these,
to leave a pressing need to learn
a little more of bees.

So in the spring, I'll do a thing
or two he left undone,
but I'd do that with Jimmy, or
with Tom, or anyone.
I always look to spring to finish
chores that got me down
in winter. I just hope a few
more springs will come around

to find me and to find the
"Winter Shaker" still inclined
to share with others what we can
of body and of mind.

But Andrew had good sense to know
that friendships too can sour,
that time hangs a persimmon on
a branch that held a flower.
So he packed up and said good bye
to comfort and to us,
and somewhere on the road he'll spend
his Christmas on a bus.
But in our hearts, he'll be with us,
and this gift we extend….
that were he not our family,
Andy still would be our friend.

Intrusion

As winter winds have wished,
my garden arbor leans,
but still content,
clematis climb and cling,
so I must to my arbor,
with songbirds' consent,
repeat repair
before the wear
of spring.

Giving In

Hoary headed
Bug eyed
Wrinkled
Multi-chinned
Hairy eared
Lost toothed
Arthritic
Asthmatic
Excuse of a vehicle

Lonely benches in the park,
Swirling snowfall,
Bark Bark Bark

Tear my trousers
Bite my shin
Break the ice
Drag me in

Not Today

Today I go down to the ships to see
If there is a ship for me;
A ship with a sail
As full as my pail
To take me out to sea.
Landlocked to labor, I milk in the barn
Of the ancient family farm.

Tear down tradition: Allow me to range.
Sailing on the tide of change.
Let my ship unbounded roam
Till I am sick of oceans
And Ireland wants me home.

Today I go down to the ships to see
If there is a ship for me,
A life beyond this county,
Free upon the bounty.
But rocks and sod
Are too long my god,
So it will never be.

We Come Again

Deep into night
Your hands are light
As tips of willow boughs
That slip around my hips
And touch my lips.
And when our mouths
Make love
And shove
Our passions
To the brink
What I may think
Undresses in the process
And your willow
Strokes
Evoke
Desire
Higher
Than before
And more
Than passion rides
The wave.
We save
Ourselves to stay the spin
To come again
In glee,
In unity.

Sweet Recall

Lay me close
To the mercy of your love
When I feel old and unsure,
Insecure.
Remind me that our love
Will sustain
Our loss,
Our pain,
Our gain.

In the cemetery
Where our love began
With the poets
And the marble
And the stand of holly trees
Please me again
With the bliss
Of our first kiss.
Let the light in your eye
Remind me that our love
Will never die.

Song Too Short

I cannot see how men can kneel
Before a crown, or kiss a ring.
I know that everything that speaks
Of me would not allow it.
I am not patriotic and I bear no creed.
I love freedom to a keen degree.
And so I pledge my allegiance
To nothing more structured than the wind.
With a forest as my cathedral
And my wife as minister in kind,
I teach my family to worship
Only nature and knowledge.
Here is a university for us to attend.
Here is eternity……live without fear.
Here is salvation if we need to be saved.

Anticipation

I drew a picture of you
last night
in my heart.
I drew the sheets
around us
and dreamed you
in fragments.

Soon you'll rise to me
down the concourse
head to high heeled toe
entire.

Before She Wakes

I peer around her swan-like neck
Across the Eider down
Through lacy islet windows
On the collar of her gown
To see a morning scout sent from
The Eastern Light Brigade
Infiltrate our encampment
From beneath our window shade.

He skirts around the yellow rose
That's fallen from the vase
And takes up his position
In the silver open space
Between the bristles of her brush
Turned up and out of place.
My lady stirs within her dreams,
A smile upon her face.

In sleep again I ventured far
Into the other camp
And made my visage known
Within the halo of their lamp.
I taunt them, but
They won't come forth,
And I awake in damp
Dream driven covers,
In a fever and a cramp.

They want that I
Would join their troupe
And stay beyond the night.
They throw their ropes around me.
They draw the slip knots tight.
But I escape again to visions
Of my morning light.

Released by dreams, I turn again
To see my lady's brush.
Her toiletries are undisturbed,
Her breathing is a hush.
The soldier smiles and turns away.
He knows where I reside.
He knows that he will find me
Every evening by her side,
But still prepared to leave her
For adventure in a dream
That makes this morning light a haze
And truth not as it seems.

The Trio

Sand slips through the glass,
hours pass,
and only love can stop the sand
and reunite your hand
with mine,
while time
can only wait
for love to
re-evaluate.

Look above, find the star
that guided us this far.
Move again in harmony,
love and you and me,
we three.

Uncle Tom is Dead

Mama pulls him to her bosom
Like a thrush
Cups her soft brown hands
Round his nappy head
Knowing that things is bound
To come to no good
Now that uncle Tom is dead.

Ed and Marcus and Lionel
Cracked as bad as the liberty bell
Polyester slaves
On a new plantation
Anti-bellum, anti-sell 'em
New things to dread
In a democratic nation
Now that uncle Tom is dead.

Martin Luther was no king
But his dream wouldn't stop
He just made sure he traveled
To the mountain top
Pulling the needle
That drags the thread
A tapestry is forming
Now that uncle Tom is dead.

But mama still can't let him go
For fear of loosing touch
The mountain top is shrouded
She tightens her clutch
She stares into the face of facts
No matter what is said
The junkies and the honkies know
That uncle Tom is dead.

Divorce

By divorce, I decree
That you be you
And I'll be me.
We'll not be us
Except in memory.

You be the wind,
And I will be the sea.
We both will be
The rising and the set,
The sun that will not
Let the past forget.

At Present

At
Present
I'm calm
But in the
Future tense
I may have become
A writer
Past perfect
Save for love of the
Past

Discontentment

You're gone.
Alone, I try to cope.
When hope
is but a thread
I take to bed.
Lights out,
and darkness in,
I sleep again,
recharging energies
I've spent
on discontent.
If I could live in light
would night
seem less a shroud?
If I could fathom me
would three
be less a crowd?
Beneath my counterpane
these pains begin.
What's left of life
is strife.
I'm giving in.

Respectful Timing

As I remodeled my old house
I came upon a mother mouse
Secured behind the safety of my wall.
I gave her fright.
She fled my sight,
But stayed close to her babies.
They were small.

I stopped to give myself a rest
And pondered on that precious nest,
And then I thought
To council with the wall.
He'd stood there many years till now,
And said it didn't matter how
He came down…
"In the Spring or in the Fall".

I put the wall back up as best
I could, to not disturb the nest,
And took my tools
To work another place.
When I came back that Fall I found
A "Thank You" note lay on the ground,
A simple smile upon the old wall's face.

Now cozy in my spruced up house
I think about that wall and mouse
And if I ever knew
I can't recall
Which one of us
Was blessed the most
By slowing down,
Or if the note
Was written by the mouse
Or by the wall.

The Promise

How brilliant must that light have been
How mystified, the three wise men
How frightened, shepherds with their sheep
How ignorant, the world asleep
How innocent, the one he chose
How common, straw and swaddling clothes
How humble, figures of the creche
How promising, the word made flesh
How difficult to understand
How undeserved, and yet how grand

Year after year the virgin birth
Reminds us of our Godly worth
As ever rings the promise clear
God's love will conquer any fear

Two Brothers and a Wife

"But age is not a polyester.
Its a virgin wool."
He often spoke in metaphors.
He used them as a tool.
"And though it wrinkles, it wears well.
It mimics human skin."
He waved his hickory walking stick
And they were off again.

She fell behind to disengage
A bramble from a fern.
She often wandered from the path
But ever would return
To arbitrate an argument
Concerning all the ways
Their mother taught them nature's lessons
In her younger days.

"In younger days, in younger days,"
He said, and now the three
Broke from the redwoods into rain
And stared out to the sea.
They stood in awe till wind and silence
Emphasized their worth.
"Lets walk our drama, arm in arm,
Out upon the surf."
"Lets wait until the weather turns around,
Till human voices wake us, ere we drown."

They heard the human voices singing
Through the mighty trees,
Through fern and bramble, wind and rain,
And pounding of the seas.
They heard their voices compromised
To nature as they bound
Into the drowning beauty
Of the sound.

Not April

Of all the months that come around
The one I least desire
Is number four, right after March,
It activates my ire.
The weather can't be counted on.
It rains and sometimes snows.
Most all my friends are still down south
And why, God only knows,
I'm back up north two months before
The season turns around.
I can't play golf or water ski
Or plant things in the ground.
The days are dark,
The empty park
Is longing for the kids.
I try to get my traction
But my attitude just skids.
The streets are bare
And everywhere
The stores are still closed up.
The birds aren't even singing.
I can't even walk my pup.
I've read my boring E-Mails twice.
I've answered all my faxes.
I've spent so much on firewood
I can't even pay my taxes.
Migration was a bit too soon.
Next year I'm coming back in June.

Night Thoughts

There's something that woke me!
A bump in the night!
At first I was dreaming,
But now I'm in fright.
There's a beast in the basement
And it's rattling it's wrath.
I won't let it out
Or get in the path
Of it's rampaging anger.
But what scares me most,
I'm lying here fearing
It might be a ghost.

The wind is a howling.
The windows are dark.
The rain is pell melling.
I'm alone in this stark
Raving mad house.
The clock just struck three.
I really would like
For someone to be
Cuddled up here beside me
At least until light.
I don't think I've courage
To last through the night.

But then I recall
By my heart's palpitation
A night light I keep there
For this situation.
I'll flip it on brightly
Till tremblings cease.
I'm falling asleep again.
Nocturnal peace.

A Letter Inside a Book

It fell
From the book as it slid from
The shelf
It spoke
Of the writer and self
And time
The cubicle built by man, so
It leaks.

Some events mock restraints
Of time,
Not subject to natural laws
Nor cause
And effect.
Some books let you know when they want to
Be read,
Some letters when they need to
Be answered.

So instead
Of a schedule we try to impose,
God knows
Only why,
Read the book when it wants to be read.
Man's way
Maybe not
The way of the book.

Sunday

She rattled in the kitchen
While poetry was read.
She baked an omelet.
I entombed the dead.
He listened to the music
Of the home, the open hearth,
And knew that he was
Grounded to this earth.

Life's ABC's

Angelically blessed,
constantly desiring
Eden's fading grandeur,
holiness intervenes, justly knowing
life makes no optimistic promise
qualifying reinstatement
so timely, unless
validating war,
x'ing youth's
zeal.

Religion

I'd sooner climb to heaven on a birch
than wrestle with the doctrine of a church,
Or spread my doubts beneath an oak
before the stroke
of lightning on the storm,
anticipating truth to form
upon a static breeze
of earth's theologies.
I'd sooner trust my fate to nature's plan
than smoke and mirrors in a bishop's hand.
Not by threats or fear or promise in the skies
will I religious freedom compromise.

Summer Thunder

I miss summer thunder,
especially at night
when silent snow grows
deeper and I fight
the urge to stir
into the cold,
outright.

If it were August
and the secret sound
of velvet marbles
wallowing around
caused me to wake
and stare,
I'd walk into the
dark and maybe
drown in
static air.

Summer thunder,
like a muffled prayer
will ever find me
listening,
aware.

Last Good-byes

Someone wants admission.
Someone will deny
the truth in the eye.
Night rolls in and
someone starts to cry,
sensing good-bye.

Despite repeated tries
love begins to winterize.
Cold rain from dark skies
glazing icy eyes,
freezing good-byes.

Carried higher in the spiral,
moving toward the day
not far away
when we recognize
the grand disguise,
too late to theorize,
final good-byes.

Toward Motherhood

A lonely walk, and yet with company;
A strain, containing pleasure still unknown.
A sudden move in pain to prove
Your journey's worth, you travel not alone.

Your fading dreams will in this love be found.
Adversities that humbled you, again
Will sound the cry that should defy
The two of you to challenge, and to win.

A task is yours to mold from common birth
Uncommon beauty. Toward a perfect form
Pursue your goal with heart and soul.
To you another trust of life is born.

Stars

As I look up into the sky
I cannot help but wonder why
The stars that flickered there last night
Today are somewhere out of sight.
Their present show is none the least.
They're shining brightly in the east.
And in another earthly spin
We'll be invited back again
To watch the dancing milky way
And constellations on display.
Oh, what a splendid treat is ours
To be so entertained by stars.

Emily Dickinson

I love Emily Dickinson
    and the grace
With which she eases death
    into his place
And prominence to smallest
    pleasures gives
And import to the purest
    forms of love.

She flirts with death and longs to
    feel his touch.
She waits for love while leaning
    on the crutch
Of words, bids both to
    mark her time,
Enticing with the beauty
    of her rhyme.

Could I with equal ease
    of pen express
The simple pleasures that
    I feel no less
Than she, then in the
    coming days
Someone might write of me with
    equal praise.

Henry and the Angels

Never having heard angel's voices before
Henry didn't know what to expect.
He stood in the middle of Iowa corn,
brilliant green, almost to his knees,
June seventeen, ten a.m., as instructed.
His clean brown Carhart bibs and
his blue plaid flannel shirt
smelled like downy lemons. He
pushed his black rubber boots more
firmly into the soft moist soil. It
was going to be a good year for corn.
From the corner of his eye he saw the
red barn and the white farm house
beyond. He felt the morning breeze
through his thinning hair.

The message had been clear and
repeated. He stretched his arms
stiffly by his sides and spread
his fingers. He had told no one
but Ruth. She advised him,
with caution, to do what he
had to do.

The ground moved beneath him.
Warm air bathed his face.
His arm pits grew wet.
Suddenly the tractor and the barn
and the house were

transported out in front of him
and then behind him
and then in front again.
He was spinning, or the farm
was spinning. Then he was
beneath the ground. He saw
the soles of his boots
and the sweet fresh roots
of the corn. Then he saw
his own body, prone around him,
six times, like human spokes,
bootless feet toward him,
head and shoulders in the distance.
Then he was transported up,
where he looked back on
his scarecrow figure.
He thought of biblical figures
called to God. He thought he
might be Jacob. Then he
thought of his cousin, Wayne,
newly reelected county sheriff.
Wayne had dealt many times
with strange acts of behavior.
How would Wayne handle this?
He tried to clear his head,
as instructed. Three nights
the voice had sounded in
his sleep, so profound as to
startle him and cause Ruth
to waken. Now the turmoil
ceased. The air was sweet,
almost no air at all. Then

the hum began to grow,
louder and higher, vibrating
through his body. Clouds
parted. Henry looked to
the sky. Immense joy ran
through his flesh. Voices
sang so high and so
beautifully that he began to
shudder and to cry. Oh, if
this was the voice of the angels,
how great must be the voice of God?

Sheltered Sin

"Repeat these few word after me,
'I solemnly do swear'
And give the bible some respect.
Quit twisting on your hair.
'that I will never spy again
or sneak or tell a lie'."
His guilty fingers gripped my arm.
I swore I wouldn't cry.
I swore it wouldn't matter if
I kept his secret safe.
I swore that I would take his ugly
action to the grave.

She never knew the lecher's sin,
nor how I gave my word.
But someone somewhere saw and knows
what I have felt and heard.

Moving Away

Don't call on the cell. I won't hear the rings
Cause I won't back down when Tom Petty sings.
I challenge my voice to sing when I speak.
I fancy the future I endlessly seek.
Where is the Eden I'm longing to reach?
Where is the ocean exposing new beach?
A void divorces the want from the need.
I'm plucking the flower while planting the seed,
Learning to live with the laughter I lost,
Fumbling at photos, counting the cost.
It just so happens it happens a lot,
Remembering items I thought I forgot.
Forgetting the items that helped me see
That all I really am is me.
Past and future form the abyss
And all there really is is "is".

I Thought Life Cruel

I thought my life was cruel to me
until I faced eternity
without my lover's rough embrace,
her manner hard, her common face.
How vast appears the empty space.

How often did the argument
full circle move to my consent.
How one we were with faults and breaks,
uncertain of the love it takes.
How over magnified the stakes.

How quickly our affection went
to tolerance when love was spent.
I need her crude persistence now
to bear the pain, or show me how.

Mockingbird

The mockingbird sings night and dawn
    a variegated song;
None of his own, but all his own,
    operatically prolonged.
And though I try to pattern him
    intently as I can
He never seems to come around
    to where he first began.

Fallout

my life is not
what I thought.
and maybe it ought
not be.
I've been caught
and what I've bought
into won't set
me free.
I'm a victim
of G.H.T.

good Harry Truman felt
he'd make it right
and he might
have in light
of the fight
but the fright
from the height
with the fallout
and blight
that was wrought
as we thought
wasn't slight
as the night
settled in.

gee, H.T.
we can see
by the doom's
fading light….we were right.

Printed in the United States
1445600001B/322-387